FOUL PLAY

Helen Chapman

SERIES CONSULTANT: LORRAINE PETERSEN

NASEN House, 4/5 Amber Business Village, Amber Close, Amington, Tamworth, Staffordshire B77 4RP

Rising Stars UK Ltd.
22 Grafton Street, London W13 4EX
www.risingstars-uk.com

Published 2009

Cover design: Burville-Riley Partnership
Illustrator: Neil Smith
Text design and typesetting: Andy Wilson for Green Desert Ltd.
Publisher: Gill Budgell
Editor: Catherine Gilhooly
Series consultant: Lorraine Petersen

British Library Cataloguing in Publication Data.
A CIP record for this book is available from the British Library

ISBN   978-1-84680-504-2

Printed by Craft Print International Limited, Singapore

CONTENTS

CHARACTERS

Ben

Ben started the All Sorts rugby team.
He is a keen and fair player.

Jonny

Jonny is new to the village and to the All Sorts.
He plays rough and to win.

Lois

Lois loves sport but is only included in the All
Sorts team because there are not enough boys!

Owen

Owen is friends with everyone, but he really looks up to Jonny and likes the way he always plays to win.

Mark

Mark plays rugby because he is good friends with Ben.

Narrator

The narrator tells the story.

Scene 1

LOSERS

Narrator The All Sorts rugby team meet
at what they call 'the clubhouse'.
But between you and me,
it's the storeroom of the church hall.

Ben Hurry up and change guys.

Lois Quick! We don't want the match to start
without us.

Mark It wouldn't matter if it did.
The result would be the same.

Lois We never win, do we?

Owen   No. I'm getting sick
of losing cvcry wcck.

Mark   Me too.

Lois   We're not even losing to good teams.

Owen   She's right. We lose to the
hopeless ones.

Mark   Yeah, they're even more hopeless than us
but they still win.

Ben   Come on guys. Stop moaning.
We'll never win if you carry on like that.

Narrator   A new player enters the storeroom ...
I mean 'clubhouse'. He's nervous
but tries not to show it by being loud
and brash.

Jonny   Hi, I'm Jonny. Coach told me
I'm playing today.

8

Ben   No way! You can't be playing.
            I haven't seen you at practice.

Jonny   Coach said it wouldn't matter.
            He said you need all the help
            you can get. So I'm here
            to give it to you.

Ben   That's so unfair.

Owen   No it's not.

Mark   Face it, Ben. We do need help.

Ben   I suppose it's okay if Coach
            said he could play.

Narrator The All Sorts introduce themselves
             to Jonny.

Jonny   Where's the rest of the team?

Ben   We're all there is.

Mark   We play seven-a-side.

Narrator Jonny looks around and counts heads.

Jonny But there's only four of you.

Owen Yeah we know.
That's why we keep losing.

Mark That and the fact we play so badly.

Lois We try and borrow three kids
from the other team
to make up the numbers.

Mark Now we only need to borrow two.

Owen So things are getting better already.

Jonny You mean you've never
had seven players?

Ben Never.

Narrator Ben nods towards Lois
as she ties up her laces.

Ben   Why do you think we have
            a girl on the team?

Jonny   So it's like that is it?

Owen   No ...

Narrator Lois interrupts.

Lois   Thank you, Owen.

Owen   ... it's not like that. It's more that
            her mum made our kit.

Mark   And stitched the numbers on the back.

Owen   And she drives us to our away matches.

Lois   Don't mind me guys!
            It's not like I have feelings
            or anything.

Narrator It's just as well.

Ben The truth is that we're the only kids around here who like sport.

Mark Rugby was an accident really.

Lois We tried to get a basketball team going.

Mark But couldn't.

Owen And a kickboxing club.

Mark But couldn't.

Ben So we started pestering everyone we met.

Lois Finally, Charlie from the garage said that if we played rugby he'd coach us.

Owen And the All Sorts were born!

Jonny Funny name.

Mark It was Charlie's idea. He said we had all sorts of skills – but not many rugby ones!

Scene 1 Losers

Jonny   So this Charlie is an ex-player is he?

Ben   He must be.

Narrator   No he's not! Charlie's never played rugby in his life! But he does watch the sports channels on TV.

Jonny   So where is he?

Mark   Charlie works in a garage.
He hardly ever gets Saturday off.

Owen   He pops back when he can
but we sort of coach ourselves.

Lois   We don't play by adult rules.
Our game is just for kids.

Jonny   So what rules do you play by?

Ben   Um ... the teams usually sort of
make them up as they go along.

Narrator Jonny stares at the All Sorts
as if they're from another planet.
He decides to make the best of things.

Jonny So how do you warm up?

Mark Put on a hoodie.

Lois Mine's a fleece.

Jonny I mean warm-up exercises.

Ben Oh right. We run ...

Mark Shuffle.

Narrator Stroll.

Ben ... around the oval.

Jonny With your coach?

Owen Sometimes.

Lois But it's hard to hear him.

Jonny You're that fast are you?

Mark No! We can't hear him
because he keeps the car window up
if it's raining.

Owen Or if he's listening to the radio.

Narrator On the pitch Jonny stands in front
of the All Sorts.

Jonny We've got to warm up.
Gentle jogging ... now!
It'll get our bodies ready for action.

Lois We'll be worn out
before the game starts.

Jonny You'll be fine. Now let's go meet
that bunch of losers.

Ben That'll be the losers
that keep winning, would it?

Jonny Not any more.
Come on, let's get 'em.

Scene 2

HEADS
OR TAILS?

Narrator	The teenage referee asks the All Sorts to call heads or tails.
Ben	I call heads.
Narrator	The referee tosses a coin to see which team will kick-off. The coin lands head up.
Lois	We won! We've finally won!
Owen	Get a grip. It's just the toss.

Lois   I know! But we've never won
the toss before. You must be
bringing us luck, Jonny.

Jonny   I guess.

Mark   What do we do now?

Owen   I dunno, but everyone's looking at us.

Lois   Oh, I haven't got my shirt on
backwards again, have I?

Ben   No, I think everyone's waiting
for us to do something.

Owen   Cool! We're important.

Jonny   Let's focus, All Sorts. We need to
work out which end
we want to attack first.

Mark   Attack?

Jonny   Yes. And we need to work out
if we're going to kick off
or let the Magpies do it.

Ben   We've never had to decide before.

Mark   He's right. We always get told
what to do.

Lois   I wish Coach was here. He'd tell us.

Owen   We could text him.

Mark   It's your call, Jonny.
You know rugby rules and stuff.

Jonny   Ben? What do you think?
It's the captain's call.

Ben   I've always wanted to do a drop kick
from the centre of the halfway line.

Jonny   Can you get the ball ten metres
from the kick off?

Lois   Is that important?

Owen   Yeah, we don't care
how far he kicks the ball.

Ben   It'd be a first to actually get near it.

Mark   I did once, remember?

Ben   Yeah, but it was after the game was over.

Narrator Jonny's losing his cool. The All Sorts are wasting time and don't seem to care.

Jonny   Listen up. Yes, it's important and yes, you should care. If Ben can't kick that far, the Magpies get to decide what to do. They can take a scrum or a throw-in on the halfway line with the feed or throw.

Narrator The kids nod as if they know what Jonny's talking about. But they don't.

Mark   None of the teams we play against
             really bother with proper rules.

Jonny   I get that, but if you don't play to win,
             what's the point?

Lois   To keep fit and have fun.

Jonny   Do you have fun when you lose?

Owen   No.

Narrator Ben decides it's time to step up
             and give his usual pep talk.

Ben   Remember All Sorts,
             the aim of the game is simple.

Narrator They chant in a sing-song voice.

Ben, Mark, Lois and Owen
             Score more points than the other team!

Scene 2 Heads or tails?

Narrator Jonny has had enough.
He strides up to the Magpies
and stares at the players.

Jonny We've got to do more than that,
All Sorts. We've got to mash 'em
and thrash 'em!

Mark He is kidding, isn't he?

Ben Doesn't sound like it to me.

Narrator Or me. In fact, Jonny looks a bit full on.

Owen He's just scaring them off.

Lois Great. Jonny's exactly what we need.

Narrator Jonny calls the All Sorts over.

Jonny I want you to watch
what I'm about to do and copy me.

Ben   What are you about to do?

Jonny   A haku. It's what the New Zealand
             All Blacks do before a game.

Lois   I've seen them on TV, they're scary.

Owen   They're big guys too.

Ben   But we're not. We'll look stupid.

Owen   We'll look even more stupid
             if we keep losing.

Mark   I'll have a go.

Lois   Me too.

Jonny   Good. It's only two verses
             and some moves.

Owen   Go on. We'll copy you.
             This'll be cool.

Jonny   Try and look mean, okay?

Narrator Jonny starts stomping his legs
             and moving his arms about.

Ben   He looks as if he's going to attack
             the other team.

Lois   That's the idea.

Narrator Jonny chants. But not in a sing-song
             voice. It's all grunts and angry shouts.

Jonny   Slap your hands against your thighs.
             Puff out your chest. Stamp your feet!

Narrator The All Sorts copy the actions.
             The Magpies looked stunned.

Mark   I've got goose bumps.

Ben   It's meant to scare the other team,
              not you.

Narrator Jonny's on a roll.

Jonny   It is death! It is death!
              It is life! It is life!

Lois   No it's not. No it's not!
              It's a game! It's a game!

Ben   Yeah, lighten up Jonny.

Owen   It's worked. Look at the Magpies.

Lois   Yeah, two of them are biting their nails.

Mark   Is that kid crying?

Ben   Laughing more like it. At all of us.

Jonny   No worries. I'll take him out first.

Narrator The All Sorts laugh, but somehow
             I don't think Jonny's joking.

Scene 3

WINNERS

Narrator The Magpies jog up and down. They're getting cold, standing around waiting for the All Sorts.

Ben What are they waiting for?

Jonny You have to choose which end.

Lois The cow field's nicer than the bus station.

Mark But there's more to look at with the bus station.

Jonny The idea is to go with the wind.

Lois   Huh?

Owen   He means you kick with the wind.
Makes it easier to score.

Narrator   Ben nods towards the cow field.

Jonny   Everyone get in your places.

Owen   We don't know where to go.

Jonny   What do you usually do?

Mark   Um ... just spread out randomly
across the field.

Narrator   The referee blows his whistle
and the game starts.

Jonny   Great kick, Ben.
Back him up All Sorts.

Narrator   Jonny runs past the other team.

Mark   Jonny's under the ball.
             He's scooping it up. He's got it.

Owen   Wow, he's fast.

Lois   He'll have to be. Two Magpies
             are waiting to dive on him.

Mark   Nah, it's okay, he's slammed
             right through them.

Owen   Was that a foul? Did the ref see?

Mark   Nah, he's on his mobile.

Owen   Just as well or Jonny would have been
             shown a yellow card.

Lois   Should we be doing something?

Owen   Yeah, let's jog around while we talk.

Mark   It looks as if Ben and Jonny
             are handling everything.

Narrator Ben races past.

Lois Hey! He's holding the ball!

Ben Did you see that?
I missed being tackled. I tricked
the defender by moving one way,
then going the other.

Narrator Jonny races past too. But he's going
in the right direction!
He shouts at Ben.

Jonny Mine!

Lois Way to go Ben! He was looking
one way and passed the ball
in the other direction!

Mark It's surprised the Magpies.

Owen Look at Jonny go!
The Magpies are
all after him.

Ben He's scored a try!

Owen   He's going to be my best mate forever!

Narrator Thanks to Jonny, the All Sorts
              score twice more. When the game ends
              they are in shock.

Ben   We won!

Mark   I know.

Ben   But ... we ... won!
              The All Sorts won.

Lois   I can't stop smiling.

Jonny   Feels great doesn't it?

Owen   Yeah.

Lois   Look at the Magpies.
              They can't believe it either.

Mark   I know.

Jonny   You've got to remember
              how good it feels to win.
              It'll help you in next week's game.

Ben   I wish Coach could have seen
my dummy pass.

Mark   What happened?

Ben   I faked a pass to Owen and it sent
the Magpie defender the wrong way.

Lois   I saw it. It was awesome.

Owen   Charlie will get a surprise
when we tell him.

Narrator   Over the next few games the All Sorts
keep winning. But not all the players
are happy.

Lois   I thought I'd be thrilled with winning
so much. But I'm over it.

Ben   Me too. I mean I loved it at first ...
but now I'm not so sure.

Mark   Before Jonny came we were really
fed up with losing.

Ben   I haven't forgotten. I want to win,
             but not *his* way.

Lois   Are you sure you're not just jealous?

Ben   If he was the best and fairest yeah,
             I would be. But I don't want to play
             so rough.

Narrator They decide to talk it over with Jonny
             as they walk back to the church hall.

Lois   Can you hang around, Jonny?
             You too, Owen. We need to talk
             about stuff.

Jonny   What's up?

Lois   I don't like the way we're playing.

Mark   I'm with Lois.

Jonny   What's your problem?
             We always win now.

Mark   It's not that we've won.
It's the *way* we've won.

Owen   What? By being better
than the other team?

Jonny   Since when is that a crime?

Ben   There's a difference between being
better and being brutal.

Lois   You're way too rough.
You mow down the other players.

Ben   It's worse than that.
You even mow us down!

Owen   That's just Jonny's game plan.

Jonny   Yeah, I don't let anyone
get between me and the ball.

Mark   You're lucky you don't give away
more penalties.

Narrator   Everyone's getting worked up
and getting louder.

Ben   Mark's right. I've seen you
target players. You run at them
as fast as you can and then
bash into them.

Jonny   You guys are clueless!
You don't even have enough brains to
thump players when the referee
isn't looking.

Lois   The All Sorts had a good name
until you came along.

Jonny   Who cares? We're a rugby team.

Owen   We should be bad and mean,
            not nice and fair.

Jonny   Don't forget, Coach asked me
            to help you losers. Well, I'm going.
            You coming Owen?

Ben   We haven't finished talking.

Owen   You can't have it both ways, guys.
            We keep winning Jonny's way
            or we go back to losing Ben's way.

Narrator Owen and Jonny leave.
            The rest of the All Sorts
            have a decision to make.

Scene 4

FAIR
OR FOUL?

Narrator Next Saturday, the All Sorts are playing
the Hawks. The referee tells the players
'No rough play'.

Jonny What's he on about? If players
can't take a punch, they shouldn't
play rugby.

Owen They should play
table tennis instead.

Jonny Good one, Owen.

Lois Give it a go, Jonny.
Just try to play fair.

Mark   Yeah, sport's about having fun,
             not thumping other players.

Jonny   Whatever.

Owen   Enough talk. Let's get out there.

Narrator Jonny and Owen sprint into play.
             Within minutes, Jonny brings down
             a Hawk with a rough tackle.

Jonny   Owen, do your stuff. Now!

Lois   Look at that! Jonny's at it already.

Mark   What happened?

Ben   He's brought down a player
             and shoved his face in the dirt.

Lois   He'll get a red card for sure.

Ben   Couldn't happen to a nicer guy.

Lois   How come you missed it, Mark?

Mark   I was watching Owen clowning about.

Narrator Jonny isn't sent to the sin bin.
The referee is too busy laughing.

Ben   I don't believe that ref!
He gets distracted too easily.

Narrator Ben knows that something odd
is going on between Jonny and Owen.

Ben   Hey Owen, what's with the clowning?

Owen   That's for me to know
and you to work out.

Ben   What's the big secret? Oh, I get it!
You're the reason Jonny
gives away so few penalties.

Mark   You're a decoy!

Owen   You bet. It's called teamwork.
This week I did my ballet moves!
Who knows what it'll be next week.

Narrator   Jonny gets up off the Hawk player.

Jonny   Owen gets the attention off me –
most of the time. If he didn't,
I'd spend the whole game in the sin bin.

Narrator   At half-time Ben comes up with a plan.

Ben   Jonny's getting worse. He's getting
away with it because of Owen.
So, Lois, you're going to shadow Jonny.

Lois   Why bother?

Ben　　Because when he fouls
　　　　you're going to make sure the ref sees.

Mark　　But if Jonny gets put in the sin bin
　　　　we're back to just four players.

Ben　　I think it's worth it.
　　　　He needs to be taught a lesson.

Narrator　They don't have long to wait.
　　　　Ten minutes later Lois sees a chance.

Lois　　Jonny's stomping all over
　　　　that Hawk player!

Mark　　Jonny's only trying to get him
　　　　out of the way.

Ben　　Fair enough too! The player's lying
　　　　over the ball on purpose. Lois, stop!

Narrator　Lois has her head down
　　　　and doesn't hear.
　　　　She charges into the ruck.

Ben   What's she doing? That's foul play!

Mark   We'll give away a penalty for sure.

Narrator Suddenly she stumbles and ends up
             on Jonny's back.

Owen   Lois! That's dangerous!

Narrator The referee wags his finger,
             shakes his head, then blows his whistle.

Jonny   Hey, Lois. If that's how you play fair,
             I'd hate to see you when you don't.

Lois   I didn't mean it. Sorry.
             I tripped over my bootlaces.

Ben   So much for my plan.
            Jonny was meant to get into trouble,
            not Lois.

Narrator   The referee doesn't send Lois
               to the sin bin. But he does ask
               for her mobile number!

Lois   He's cute, isn't he. And he's in Year 9.

Narrator   After another few minutes of play
               Jonny bulldozes head on into
               a Hawk player. Play stops. Again!

Lois   Eeew. That crack sounded like
            a bone breaking.

Mark   Nah, it's just two gorillas meeting
            head on.

Owen   Jonny's got to stop this macho act.
            Hey, is he okay?

Mark   Don't think so, he's really hurt himself.
That was one foul too many.
We'd better help him.

Narrator The boys help Jonny off the pitch.

Jonny   Thanks for nothing, Owen.

Owen   You're out of control mate.
I can't be a decoy all the time.

Narrator Jonny doesn't train or play
the following week. As the All Sorts
are in the storeroom – er – 'clubhouse',
they make a surprise discovery.
They actually miss Jonny!

Ben   Jonny taught us these hamstring stretches.

Mark   And we're loads fitter.

Owen   If you think about it, he held
the team together. We were
getting fed up losing, remember?

Lois   I thought he'd come watch us play.
         But he hasn't.

Ben   I wonder where he disappeared to.

Narrator   They hear a whistle behind them.

Jonny   Hi guys.

Mark   Where have you been?

Jonny   Don't laugh. I've taken up boxing.

Owen   What? So you let off steam
          with a punch bag now.

Jonny   Yeah, check out my moves.
          I float like a butterfly, sting like a bee.

Ben   So does this mean
          no more foul play?

Jonny   Not from me. But I'd keep
          an eye on Lois if I was you!

IN THE
CHATROOM ...

After the All Sorts beat another team, there is an online debate.

The Local SPORTS LOCKER

Tell us what you think!

Message board: All Sorts versus Tigers

Sat 4.30 p.m.
Game on! We are the best rugby team in town. I've just come back from the game. Wicked! What a great new player. 😊

Sat 4.45 p.m.
Great new player? Total cheat more like! Your team used to have a good name, but not anymore. 😞

- Which message was posted by a Tigers' fan and which message was posted by an All Sorts' fan? How can you tell?

ROLE PLAY ...

Split into two groups of three. One group takes on the roles of Jonny, Owen and the Coach. The other group takes on the roles of Ben, Lois and Mark.

- Jonny's group must think of arguments in favour of winning using any tactics – fair or foul.

- Ben's group must think of arguments in favour of fair play.

- Remember to give reasons to support your point of view.

- Hold a debate by taking it in turns to present your point of view.

- After the debate, stop being your character. Now, hold a vote on what *you* think is the most important: winning or playing fair.

MATCH REPORT ...

- *Look again at Scene 4.*

- *Pretend you work for a newspaper. Write a report of what happened in the game.*

- *Remember to include all the action and to think of a good headline.*

- *The words in this box might help you:*

foul
cheat
bad tackle
clowning around
referee wasn't looking
should have been a penalty

ASTRO-MAN
TOFFEE NOSE
BURIED ALIVE!
FOUL PLAY
PLANE CRAZY
YARD
DUMPED!
STEP WARS

Interact plays are available from booksellers or
www.risingstars-uk.com

For more information please call 0800 091 1602

RISING STARS